THE ITALIAN REAL ESTATE INDUSTRY

Gabriele Fraschini

ISBN: 1542636639
ISBN 13: 9781542636636
Library of Congress Control Number: 2017902947
CreateSpace Independent Publishing Platform
North Charleston, South Carolina

This book is dedicated to Tommaso Fraschini.
I have the honor of being his father.

CONTENTS

INTRODUCTION

The Italian real estate industry began to take form in the mid-1990s as a result of extremely favorable economic and social conditions. Several factors contributed to the growth of this new business sector. For instance, during that time, property prices in Italy were considerably lower than in other European countries. Moreover, there was a need to develop the large urban areas that had been abandoned by the government. Referred to as vacant sites, these carried low inflation rates and large amounts of fund availability for property projects of varying scales, including the construction of anything from basic buildings to more complex developments. The possibility of the euro becoming Italy's common currency not only led to the country's financial stability but also made investment universally more appealing.

Today, the real estate industry in Italy includes approximately seventeen thousand service companies with more than thirty-five thousand staff. The employment rate is far above 7.9 percent, added value stands at 11.1 percent, and the net production totals €16 billion. Financial services appear to have the greatest success, while facility management and production services come in a close second. If you include the construction industry in the real estate industry, then the GDP percentage is catapulted to more than 10 percent.

The Italian Real Estate Industry Association, Assoimmobiliare (www.assoimmobiliare.it), recently audited 304 transformation projects taking place in urban areas. They found that 15 percent of them were entertainment and shopping centers with an average surface area of approximately fourteen thousand square meters, and €103 million altogether was being invested in them. Logistics centers made up 16 percent of the projects; on average, they had a 400,000-square-meter area, and €163 million was being invested in them. Finally, mixed-use complexes made up 38 percent of the developments; they had an average surface area of fifty-two thousand square meters, and €555 million was being invested in them. Forty-seven percent of the projects were located in the northwest region of the country, 18 percent were in the northeast, 20 percent were in the middle of the country, and 15 percent were in the south.

There are 3.9 million people living in Milan, and according to the latest statistics from the Milan Chamber of Commerce, the city has 336,593 businesses. Milan accounts for 42.3 percent of Lombardy's enterprises and 6.5 percent of the national total. The per capita GDP exceeds €34 thousand, and Milan produces more than 10 percent of Italy's GDP.

Innovation has always been the main focus in Milan. In fact, the city houses 15 percent of the high-tech companies in Italy. Foreign trade is at the core of its manufacturing activities. In 2004, Milan accounted for more than 25 percent of Italian imports and 13 percent of exports. In addition, most of the major banks and insurance companies, both foreign and domestic, are based in Milan. The city is, without a doubt, the unrivaled capital of the Italian real estate industry.

In recent years, the Italian real estate market has shown favorable signs of recovery from 2008. Approximately €3 billion were invested in it in the first half of 2015—an increase of 66 percent from 2014—and, at present, it is showing no signs of slowing down. The majority of this interest in Italian property stems from foreign investors who never previously invested in Italy. These include Asian institutional investors, American private-equity investors, sovereign wealth funds from the Middle and Far East, and European family offices. Italian investors generally look for more diversified portfolios, which encourages asset managers to offer specialized and sophisticated investment products.

A five-year plan seeking to invest €356 million in developing the outskirts of Milan is currently underway. Although up to half of the budget has yet to be found for the project, it remains the objective of Mayor Giuseppe Sala. Indeed, it was the promise he made during his electoral campaign. The five main districts involved are Bovisa, Gallaratese, Corvetto, Adriano, and Giambellino. All large areas, these regions make up more than half of the outskirts of Milan, and they are the ones in most need of development. The plan is expected to improve streets, rebuild social housing complexes, create theaters for children, build training centers for entrepreneurial activities, build new schools, and reinforce public transport services. The goal is to establish all of this by June 2021.

Milan's city council is currently considering how funding for the project can be obtained without burdening the people with taxes. According to Sala, €10 million will come from the Matteo Renzi-led government, while €70 million will come from new governments. One of the major obstacles to this strategy is the fact that the Renzi government is no longer in operation; of course, this shifts the responsibility to Prime Minister Paolo Gentiloni. The remaining €100 million will be sourced from the sale of Serravalle shares.

Growth in the real estate industry appears to have been steady during the past three years. If this trend continues through 2017, that will make it four years of growth. The industry has been in a crisis for slightly more than eight years now, and property values have significantly declined. Average prices have seen a 30 percent reduction, with less attractive suburban locations experiencing the worst of it at 50 percent. During the past two years, a renewed interest in real estate has opportunely led to more transactions and mortgage applications.

According to preliminary information from CBRE (www.cbre.com), €8.9 billion was invested in nonresidential real estate in 2016—9 percent more than in 2015. The office segment appears to have performed the best throughout the year with €3.5 billion in investments. The retail sector followed with €2.48 billion in investments.

European elections have the potential to influence the market's stability; however, investors continue to be optimistic when it comes to the Italian real estate sector. More than three years ago, when American giant Blackstone paved the way for the return of large international investments to Italy, many investors launched several deals. Companies like Schroder's are looking to invest in cities with significant growth potential. They are carefully evaluating infrastructure developments and demographic transformation and are currently concentrating on Rome and Milan.

At the moment, Schroder's manages €6 billion in assets throughout continental Europe. In Italy, they are looking at all sectors, from offices to logistics to retail.

1

OWNING REAL ESTATE

In Italy, the assorted rights in regard to real estate assets are as follows:

- **Absolute Freehold or Full Ownership**
  This gives a person the sole right to fully dispose of the property. It is the broadest right that can be held in real estate.
- **Right to Build**
  This gives a person the right to construct and maintain a building underneath or on top of another person's property, granted for a certain period of time. After the expiration date, the landowner is entitled to take possession of the building. It also provides the landowner the right to sell the title for the underlying land.
- **Beneficial Interest**
  This gives a person the right to relish another person's real estate for a certain period of time. If the beneficiary is an individual, this cannot be longer than their life span; if the beneficiary is a legal entity, this cannot be longer than thirty years. The beneficiary is entitled to use the real estate in the same way that the owner does. This includes granting leases and collecting interest as long as the property's original use is maintained.

- **Right of Use**
  This gives a person the right to use real estate for the purpose of meeting his or her needs and those of his or her immediate family.
- **Long Lease**
  This provides a person the same rights as the property's owner. He or she pays rent to the bare owner and must improve the property. If a certain amount is paid, he or she has the right to become a full owner. The length of the lease cannot be less than twenty years and may be perpetual. This right is exceptionally rare in common practice.
- **Co-Ownership and Condominium**
  Property rights, which include the right to full ownership of real estate, may be co-owned by two or more people, legal entities, or companies. Co-ownership can also be available for a condominium. While this right typically relates to housing, it can likewise relate to shopping malls where various people own several different units.

  Condominium members have the right to co-own the common assets that are of similar value to their respective interests in relation to the value of the building or whole real estate complex. Co-ownership rights, expressed with interest, are calculated on the basis of 1/1000 and then listed in a millesimal chart. The quota is a representation of the value of the voting rights of each condominium member. The co-owners are permitted to adopt condominium regulations (which is mandatory with more than ten owners) that enforce governing rules on the use of the common areas, the management of the condominium, and the distribution of applicable expenses.

  Co-ownership rights can only be transferred with a transfer of the owner's interest.
- **Restrictions**
  Typically, no restrictions are associated with the purchase of real estate by foreign investors. However, when an investment

is through the purchase of shares in a corporate vehicle, the foreign ministry may implement some restrictions. In rare instances, mandatory preemption rights are imposed on real estate assets.

Other Property Rights

Mortgages, Pledges, and Privileges

A mortgage—the most common form of real estate security—is an in rem security that places pressure on real estate assets. It incorporates the land, the buildings that have been constructed on it, and the fixtures that make up those buildings. The creditor who holds a receivable that has been secured by a mortgage can begin an expropriation in regard to the burdened property. Once the sale has been enforced and the beneficiary of the mortgage has been paid, the profit is dispensed among the creditors.

A mortgage may burden the right to full ownership of real estate, but it can also be established over other real estate rights, such as rights to bare ownership, rights to build, and beneficial interests.

It is possible for a mortgage to be based on a voluntary deed of the debtor or of a third party over its properties; however, in certain instances, the law permits a creditor to establish a mortgage over the debtor's properties, particularly the right granted to the seller of a real estate asset to secure the payment of the price.

Mortgages must be carried out by deed in the presence of a notary public and be filed with the appropriate real estate register in order to be validly established. Judicial awards and orders of payment from the court permit the creditor to establish a mortgage for the debtor's properties. The mortgage will be fully established once it has been filed with the real estate register.

A property can have more than one mortgage on it, and when it does, any claim regarding the credit secured by the senior mortgage is given priority over those regarding receivables secured by any junior mortgages.

A mortgage does not terminate automatically if a transfer of properties takes place and those properties are burdened by the same; the mortgage follows the property and stays the same.

A pledge is different from a mortgage: although it is an in rem security, it doesn't burden real estate assets but only movable assets. Lastly, a range of claims collectively referred to as privileges have statutory priority over the claims of any other creditor in relation to the proceeds of a debtor's property—the state for direct and indirect taxes, for example.

In principle, pledges take precedence over privileges over movables, and special privileges over real estate assets, and immovable properties over mortgages.

Easements
An easement consists of an encumbrance burdening a property to provide another property, owned by a separate person or entity, a direct advantage. An easement requires an existing relationship between two properties, the benefited one and the burdened one, without any prejudice toward the possibility of setting up reciprocal easements between the two burdened properties.

A simplified list of the most common type of easements includes rights of way, which could be with vehicles and/or pedestrians and which typically permit passage between part of one property and another, such as electric pipeline easements, gas pipeline easements, and so on.

As they are in rem rights, third parties can enforce easements, and they do not terminate if the properties affected by the same are transferred; they follow the property and stay with the same.

Generally, an easement is established through a contract between the owners of two properties; however, one can also be established through judicial awards or an administrative measure. The agreements that put an easement in place must be in writing and, in order to be effective with third parties, must be executed by a notarial deed and filed with the real estate registers.

It is also possible to alter a property by setting up personal rights over that property in favor of an individual or legal entity rather than in favor of another real estate asset. These rights would not be deemed in rem rights but personal rights, which are not enforceable through third parties and have no effect if the affected property is transferred.

For an investor, it is advisable to determine whether any easements will have an adverse effect upon the target property or whether the latter property is allowed an easement in its favor. Consideration should also be given to whether the application of a planned investment, such as the improvement of a shopping mall or the development of land, requires the establishment of easements in favor of the property that has been purchased.

2

REAL ESTATE ASSETS CLASSIFICATION

Real estate assets can be classified by the following destinations of use:

- Residential
- Offices
- Commercial
- Industrial
- Specific

Residential

Residential real estate comprises a type of property constructed for individuals or families to occupy in a nonbusiness capacity. The residential sector in Italy accounts for 75 percent of the real estate industry. The average transaction value for residential real estate is €150,000.

The three main indicators to take into consideration when evaluating whether the residential market will grow or slow down are the number of transactions, the average time for a sale, and the discounts.

Residential real estate in Italy includes the following types of property:

- **Flat Buildings**
  Approximately half of all properties in Italy are flats. This is due to the high demand for housing in and around its major cities. These buildings are typically five to seven floors in height, with balconies and flat roofs to provide space on the outside of each apartment. The ground floor is generally leased for commercial use, such as a restaurant, bar, or shop. The first floor is often undesirable due to its proximity to the busy streets; because of this, it is often used as an office.
- **Terraced Houses (*Casa a Schiera*)**
  Italian suburbs and small villages are often cluttered with quaint, tiny streets of traditional terraced homes and a few detached properties. Terraces can be exceptionally long, but they are not very wide. They typically cover several floors, and each one has its own courtyard or small garden. Parking spaces are limited, as the small streets were not built with cars in mind.
- **Villas (*Villetta*)**
  Today, the term *villetta* is used to describe any small, detached house. In the past, it was traditionally used to describe a retreat for the wealthy or a country home. These huge houses allowed their owners to escape city life without having to forfeit the luxuries they were accustomed to. Modern villas vary in shape and size. They are generally built in the Mediterranean or Tuscan style, and many still have the Spanish architectural influence that previously inspired many Italian mansions. Villas tend to have gabled or flat red-tile roofs, tall arched windows, and a vast amount of outside space.
- **Chalets**
  Chalets are very common in the Italian Alps. Their entire structure is built out of wood, and they feature open-plan living and exposed beams. Chalets are encircled with wraparound balconies as well as ornately designed railings. They are constructed this way because of the various seasons and accompanying (often

extreme) weather conditions; they are capable of withstanding cold temperatures and high winds, trapping heat during the colder months and keeping the home cool during the summer. Chalets are used as residential homes, but they are more commonly used to accommodate skiers on holiday.

Residential real estate in Italy had a moderate increase in price from the latter portion of the 1990s until 2007–2008. The country had not experienced a real estate bubble to the same extent that other European countries—such as Ireland and Spain—had. The first sign of crisis in the Italian real estate market occurred after investments in the construction industry began to plummet in 2006. This had a major effect on the nonresidential sector, too. The instability of the financial structure of Italian construction companies compared with their European counterparts caused an increase in defaults. This, combined with the major funding gap in the banking industry, forced the country's banks to manufacture a credit crunch for the real estate industry. One of the repercussions was that investments in 2007 reached their peak that year before suffering a constant decline, with no sign of the crash being reversed.

Despite this unusual phenomenon, the circumstantial and more than proportional decline in sales numbers caused the accumulation of approximately half a million unsold houses. In fact, the amount of real estate sales in general has decreased during the past decade. The Italian market is considered vendor driven, and properties are sold when sellers are satisfied with the price buyers are willing to pay. The market suffers from having what is referred to as a "double-dip" nature. After its collapse in 2008, it began to stabilize between 2009–2011; however, the escalating credit crunch on the buyers' side, as well as Italian banks narrowing their funding gap, caused another recession in 2012. Thankfully, information from recent years appears to show the onset of a recovery. This is probably due not only to a price drop but also to real estate becoming more affordable and credit conditions improving.

Today, residential real estate is still the main development in Italy. In 2015, Compagnia Investimenti Sviluppo (www.cis-vr.it) built a €350 million project. The same company also promoted the regeneration project Forum Mondadori in the historic center of Mantova. A €70 million investment was attached to the project. AEDES Siiq S.p.A partnered with Gefim and constructed a €300 million development in Finale Ligure, on the coast of Liguria. The project boasted both residential and commercial facilities.

Offices

Offices are available for investment only in Milan and Rome—there are no opportunities for substantial investment or returns in the rest of the country. The two main indicators to take into consideration when evaluating whether the residential market will grow or slow down are the quality of vacant offices and the amount of take-up (square meters leased in the previous year).

Commercial

The commercial sector can be divided into the categories of food and no food. No food comprises factory outlets, shopping centers, and high street retail.

The commercial real estate sector in Milan attracted considerable interest from foreign wealth funds throughout 2015; interest from investors in Italy's business capital continued in 2016 and is expected to sustain throughout 2017. Several historic buildings in Milan have attracted foreign investments due to structural reforms, low rates, and international liquidity. In January 2015, the State Oil Fund of the Republic of Azerbaijan (SOFAZ) reached a deal to purchase historic property in the center of Milan. SOFAZ purchased the Palazzo Turati for €97 million. This was the fund's first investment in Italian real estate. At the end of December 2015, Qatar Investment Authority bought another historic building in the subsidiary of BNP Paribas in the center of Milan. China and the United States have also been instrumental: in the summer of 2014, one of China's most prominent privately owned groups, Fosun, purchased the former headquarters of the Italian bank UniCredit. All of these investments have assisted, and will continue to assist, with Italy's economic growth.

Commercial real estate investment had increased by €8 billion by the end of 2015. This was a 45 percent improvement from 2014. Out of that €8 billion, €4 billion was invested in Milan's metropolitan area. Foreign and local investment in the Italian real estate market increased the confidence of those potential investors who remained skeptical about investing in the Italian market.

Italy has historically been considered a safe country due to its ability to remain in good financial standing even when other European companies experience economic ruin. The Italian commercial real estate market is continuing to stabilize, and as it does, it is becoming more and more attractive to foreign investors.

Factory Outlets
There are not too many factory outlets in Italy. However, this sector is very interesting from an investor's point of view, as indicated by the Percassi Group's (www.percassi.it) acquisition of the Soratte Outlet (www.soratteoutlet.it) in December 2016.

Shopping Centers
At present, the Italian market is dominated by structures of less than forty thousand square meters. It has 762 shopping centers, and 82 percent of them are at BB, B, and C level. Their vacancy rate is high but stable, ranging from 12.2 percent to 20 percent for C-class centers in comparison to the 2.7 percent of AAA and a 6 percent reduction from the 7 percent of AA. If these centers desire growth, they are going to have to change their strategy. An easy resolution would be for some of them to shut down, but a lot of them could potentially renew their profit in several different ways.

At the end of 2015, seven new retail centers opened, and three of them belonged to the AA category: the GrandApulia in Foggia (www.

grandapulia.it), the Arese Shopping Center near Milan (www.centroil-centro.it), and the Roncadelle Shopping Center in the province of Brescia (www.elnosshopping.info). Five of the new centers belonged to the BB category. In the shopping center commercial real estate sector, there is room for investment in terms of added value; a number of shopping centers have been purchased as a result. The challenge that Italian consultancy firms face when they attempt to initiate investments from international companies who are interested in the country is finding the right solutions to solidify those investments.

High Street Retail
In the compelling world of retail, the high street is becoming a hot spot for major investors. Despite the financial crisis, the strenuous economic climate that is putting others out of business has only marginally affected luxury goods and high street retailers. Within this context, Milan has been successful in maintaining its fashion capital reputation, with high-end international retailers constantly opening (or about to open) new stores in the area. Existing retailers are reporting that their stores on Milan high streets are doing better than those at any other location.

Although Italy is currently experiencing challenging times as a result of structural and unpredictable economic problems, it still holds its place as the fourth-largest GDP in the European Union. It is also at an advantage because of its large and diverse potential consumer base, which includes businesses, wealthy residents, students, and fashion and design tourists. Among the most prominent attractive cross-border retail destinations in Europe, Italy stands in fifth place. For the top one hundred luxury brands, it ranks third. There is no sign of decline in new openings in Milan, which means that the city is still in need of both Italian and international retailers. When evaluating retail values, Corso Vittorio Emanuele has been compared to Sloane Street in London, and Via Montenapoleone features among the top ten luxury streets in Milan.

During the past few years, Milan has seen remarkable interest in its high street retailers of differing prices and standing. COS (www.cosstores.com) purchased a unit in the former Armani store on Corso Venezia, and Hackett opened a large unit in the same area. This is due to the growing structured property portfolio strategy that retailers have been pursuing in the hopes of maximizing revenue in the best location.

Via Montenapoleone, located in the heart of Milan's Quadrilatero della Moda, is the fourth-most-expensive street in Europe. This positions the luxury street at the top of the global retail property hierarchy. In addition, Milan has good positioning in the total rental price range; it offers an assortment of locations, suitable for all budgets and market standings. For instance, Corso Vittorio Emanuele is in the €3,000–€6,000 rental bracket, while other streets have prime rents estimated as sitting below the €3,000 threshold.

Milan's city center is one of the most active retail scenes in Italy and in Europe, with approximately 500,000 square meters of retail space. According to recent research, it contains a total of nine prominent high streets that all feature most prominently in the retail industry: Corso Vercelli, Via Manzoni, Via Montenapoleone, Corso Buenos Aires, Corso Venezia, Corso Vittorio Emanuele II, Galleria Vittorio Emanuele II, Via Dante, and Via Torino. These nine streets also feature the greatest commercial and historic relevance in Milan.

According to data from the Italian Council of Shopping Centers (CNCC), the end of 2016 brought 272,000 square meters of new retail space in shopping centers. This highlights the renewed importance of a sector that had been abandoned during the real estate crisis. Future investments could initiate as much as €200 million being pumped into the sector.

Shopping centers that opened in 2016 include Il Centro near Milan (www.centroilcentro.it). It continues to be a huge success and has been responsible for introducing several new brands into the Italian market. Scalo Milano (www.scalomilano.it), which also opened in the Milan area in 2016, is another smaller shopping center of only thirty thousand square meters, but it shows great innovation, and a large section of it is dedicated to design. Activity in this area has continued, as well as investments in Southern Italy. In fact, investing in shopping centers is an important trend in the Italian real estate industry and the economy in general. It allows the country to recover industrial land and return to the city entire portions of land that are paying high urbanization fees.

The CNCC's Italian Shopping Centers Association website (www. cncc.it) contains a comprehensive list of the main shopping centers in Italy. Among other activities, they assist shopping centers in relocating to the inner cities, which is what typically takes place in other European countries. This is a major project: not only is it going to create more shopping centers, it will also assist in the building of more social hubs. These facilities will in turn assist in the redevelopment of entire neighborhoods and the creation of real communities. It is a way to revive parts of the city that have been abandoned or just need improvements—and a strategy that is going to be used more and more often in Europe.

There was a reduction in sales in the summer of 2016, and this became an issue of concern as shopping center sales declined almost 3 percent in three months, from July through September. There was also a slight reduction in sales between January and October. The forecast for 2017 looks positive; a number of new commercial openings are on the way. One of them will be the CityLife Shopping District in Milan.

Industrial
The industrial sector can be divided into light industrial and heavy industrial. It is not an active investment sector in Italy as of January 2017.

Specific Destinations of Use
Health Care Real Estate Sector
An increase in demand for investments in traditional core properties has led to more focus on alternatives, the health care real estate

sector being one of them. This sector includes clinics and hospitals as well as general and local doctors' offices. Research has indicated that approximately 15 percent of funds is currently being allocated to such noncore assets, with an estimated 90 percent of investors planning to increase these allocations during the next five years.

Interest in the health care property market is growing across Northern Europe. Reasons for this include the rising expenses associated with health care and an aging population. What this means is that health care property has a very low volatility, making it similar to an annuity investment. Research conducted by Your Care Consult discovered that €1.4 billion in health care transactions were conducted in Europe in 2016. With health care growing in popularity, several other sectors have begun attracting strong returns for investors, too.

Activity appears to be slower in Southern Europe, and countries such as Spain and Italy are not attracting the same amount of investment because of their historically low demands and investment volumes.

Cinema Real Estate Sector
In 2016, the Italian government announced that it would be increasing funding in the film industry by 60 percent. Exact figures are set at more than €150 million. The changes will be initiated in 2017, and Italy can expect to see government support increase in this area to €427 million per year.

Previously, funds for cinema were withdrawn from a single government pot that had been put aside for theater, opera, cinema, and music. The film and audiovisual industries are now going to have their own separate fund. Furthermore, productions are going to be supported based upon past artistic and financial achievements. This will mirror the practice in France, whose government's support of cinema is acknowledged internationally.

Italy's minister of cultural heritage and activities and tourism, Dario Franceschini, has stated that the government plans to modernize its commitment to cinema. Priority will be given to writers and young filmmakers, and up to 15 percent of the new fund will go toward supporting first and second productions. Tax credits will increase to attract foreign investment in Italy and will likewise apply to Italian independent producers. There will also be strong incentives for those who invest in new cinema buildings as well as for those who are preserving film libraries and cinemas throughout Italy.

High Street Retail
There has been significant investment in high street retail during recent years. In 2015, M&G Investments purchased a corporate entity that held a major high street retail asset in central Milan. This asset became a part of M&G's main European property strategy. Today, the 3,745-square-meter development is one of the elite commercial locations in Milan's city center and houses an infusion of national and international retailers. It opened in the spring of 2015, and it became one of the largest and most distinguished retail units in central Milan. Prominent European fashion retailer Teddy S.p.A. (www.teddygroup.com) now has two leases; the property houses the company's headquarters, where it operates flagship stores under its Terranova and Calliope brands. Deals such as this show how high-quality developments in Italy can attract international players on both the leasing and the investment side.

Logistics Sector
The logistics sector has reported increased interest from foreign buyers who are seeking buyers in the Italian market. This activity is expected to continue, especially for core properties, as reflected within the yield compression for prime assets in major cities. Key elements of the logistics market are built-to-suit projects, the e-commerce evolution, 3PLs, and retailers' demand, particularly in the food sector.

For the first three quarters of 2016, the occupational market continued to report a positive trend; its volume doubled compared with the same period in the previous year. Tenants still showed a strong interest in Lombardy, where almost half the activity was recorded. The

Emilia Romagna region came in a close second, with take-up mainly concentrated in the provinces of Bologna and Piacenza. All transactions in these areas were more than ten thousand square meters and represented 90 percent of the total grade-A space transacted. In the present market, where the grade-A vacancy rate is low, built-to-suit projects are experiencing a positive trend, covering 40 percent of the yearly take-up. Occupiers prefer to have tailor-made innovative spaces in the prime logistic hubs. The majority of demand comes from the retail sector, particularly from food companies, which require temperature-controlled warehouses, and from 3PLs, which follow e-commerce growth.

Investment volumes for industrial assets are lower than they have been for the last two years; however, international investors continue to show interest. They account for more than 60 percent of the volume transacted, mostly for properties located in the north of Italy.

The main drivers for the occupational market are location and quality. From an investment perspective, Italy remains one of the most interesting countries in the eurozone. Due to new projects being developed for major companies, Rome's logistics market keeps gaining more and more attention.

Offices

The office market in Italy maintains a positive trend on both the investment and the occupational side. Interest in core products continues to increase, and as a result, offices in core locations of major cities have seen a rental growth and yield compression.

The Milan office market take-up in the first three quarters of 2016 was almost 30 percent higher than the amount from 2015. This was mainly driven by large deals of more than ten thousand square meters, which represented 27 percent of the total yearly absorption. Today, the market confirms that tenants prefer to relocate to iconic buildings and high-quality spaces: the largest transactions (larger than five thousand square meters) have been for new grade-A buildings with green certification or for properties that are under construction.

After a temporary halt, the development market has restarted, and this will likely cause an increase in the short-term supply. Despite a large pre-let transaction, the office market in Rome recorded a take-up volume higher than values recorded during the same period of the past two years. In contrast to Milan, the market for new developments remains static; this is due to the lack of international developers and primarily led by pre-let agreements.

The office sector is still the highest-performing asset class, representing approximately 40 percent of the total Italian real estate investment volume, and it therefore confirms the growth trend that has been recorded during the last few years. Foreign investors are still dominating this area, and pressure is mounting on prime core assets. Milan is ahead in terms of volume, covering almost 60 percent of the total volume within the sector. However, prime products in Rome still attract significant interest from investors.

It is predicted that the occupational market will maintain its positive trend: large one-off transactions will influence year-end figures, and investors will continue with their interest in investing in Italy.

3

REAL ESTATE BUSINESS MODELS

Property Companies

The property company business model—adopted by companies like Grosvenor (www.grosvenor.com) and Beni Stabili (www.benistabili.it)—is based on the practice of investing in existing real estate assets during an extended period of time. These assets generate returns both from income return and appreciation of the asset.

In Italy, listed real estate investment companies are known as Società di Investimento Immobiliari Quotate (SIIQs), and they are the Italian vehicles that resemble real estate investment trusts (REITs). SIIQs must be formed as joint-stock companies, and their shares must be listed on a regulated stock exchange of a European Union member state. They must be domiciled for income tax purposes in Italy or in another European member state.

Italy eased the rules for SIIQs (or REITs) in 2014 with the so-called Unlock Italy Decree. Signed by Prime Minister Renzi, it was designed to put vehicles' tax-efficient status on equal footing with those of France and Spain while also bringing them in line with the country's closed-end property funds.

As of January 2017, Italy has a total of eight SIIQs. The central ones are as follows:

- **Coima Res**

  In 2016, Coima Res (www.coimares.com) raised €215 million in a successful IPO that would hopefully lead to the Italian listed real estate sector finally seeing some growth. The listed real estate sector is now set to grow following the introduction of the REIT method in Italy. According to the European Public Real Estate Association (EPRA), the listing may initiate the stirrings of a renaissance in Italy's small listed real estate industry. The Coima Group has developed, invested in, and managed five million square meters of commercial real estate in Italy during its forty-year history and now manages a total of more than €5 billion in assets.

  The Milan-based investor-developer had a bumper year in 2015, completing a €2 billion sale to Qatar Investment Authority (QIA) of Porta Nuova. The office-led, mixed-use scheme was developed with Hines Italia in Milan. Manfredi Catella, the former head of Hines Italia and the current head of Coima, led the buyout of the joint venture with Hines, with the financial backing of QIA. Hines subsequently reintroduced its presence in Italy to feed the country's demand for new developments. Coima is now doing the same: in January 2016, it acquired a tower project as part of its expansion of Porta Nuova. In May, the asset manager spun off the development unit as a new REIT—Coima Res—dedicated exclusively to institutional investors. The offering, which was backed by QIA's sovereign wealth fund, was downsized from an initial planned volume of €330 million but nevertheless represented the biggest success that the country's listed property sector had seen in years. Shares were placed among several major institutional investors from Europe and the United States.

- **IGD**

  IGD (www.gruppoigd.it) has a €2.9 billion investment portfolio with properties in eleven regions throughout Italy. It also has a branch in Romania, where it owns a chain of fourteen shopping centers known as Winmarkt. The main function of IGD is to purchase and manage properties, its primary investment being in malls and hypermarkets. The company is engaged in meticulous business strategies to maximize its profit.

  In 2008, IGD became the first company to acquire SIIQ status as a result of its superior business model. Its portfolio consists almost exclusively of hypermarkets and galleries located in medium- to large-size shopping malls. In Italy, these buildings are distributed throughout the country, from Piedmont to Sicily, in eleven different regions.

- **Beni Stabili**

  Those who run Beni Stabili (www.benistabili.it) are known as the forerunners in the Italian real estate industry. They boast assets of €3.9 billion. They own properties throughout Italy, in all major cities in the northern and southern regions. Their investment portfolio consists of offices, and they apply customized investment strategies to ensure that they maximize their profits and create value for their partners, shareholders, and clients.

  The team at Beni Stabili apply the best solutions to their developments to ensure that all the buildings they choose to invest in are a cut above the rest. They recently acquired full control of Revalo (www.revalo.it), another forerunner in the real estate industry, whose main focus is on managing property portfolios and advisory and facility services. They made the decision to integrate Revalo into their group so that they could control the entire real estate value chain of its portfolio and thus include it in the evolution of the Beni Stabili portfolio. Most importantly, Beni Stabili intends to pursue a new strategy that will focus on further improving the quality of services aimed at tenants, promoting collaboration and efficiency. This transaction provides the company the opportunity to internalize a superior facility and property service, which represents a main factor of success in today's highly competitive real estate market.

Founded in 1904, Beni Stabili has been listed on the Milan Stock Exchange since 1999 and on the Paris Stock Exchange since 2010. In 2007, it became part of the French group Foncière des Régions, a major European property player. Beni Stabili has operated as an SIIQ since January 2011.

- **CBRE Group, Inc.**
  CBRE Group, Inc. is an American commercial real estate company with headquarters in Los Angeles, California. As of its successful 2011 bid to acquire part of ING, CBRE was the world's largest real estate investment manager. CBRE was ranked at 363 in the Fortune 500 in 2014 and was the highest-ranked company in the real estate sector.

  CBRE Global Investors—an affiliate of CBRE Group, Inc.— entered Italy in 2003; it has twenty staff members in the country, managing €1.1 billion of assets. The company has been looking more favorably on the real estate market during the past twelve months, as the market is offering relative value as well as rental growth potential at a time when most core European markets are some steps farther in their recovery process.

Property-Management Companies

The business model employed by property-management companies is based on their capability to generate returns in joint ventures with other investors through two things: returns on assets and profit from services. It is further based on the fact that cross-border investments are becoming more and more important in the real estate industry. When a real estate fund decides to invest in Italy, they have to decide whether to appoint a dedicated company to look after their asset or identify a reliable partner who can take care of the property's management for them. The first solution has two problems: first, setting up a team requires time, and if the investment is short term, that could be an issue; second, the cost associated with property-management services requires a large investment, and it may be uneconomical to set up a property-management company for a limited investment.

There is room in the market for companies that can supply a full array of real estate services, such as asset management, property building management, facility management, and property construction management. The international investor, as a condition, requires the joint venture to grant all such services to the property-management company. The specific services offered are as follows:

- **Asset Management**
  Asset management is the service with the highest added value, for it governs all other activities and generates return for the investors.
- **Property Building Management**
  Property building management is the operational implementation of the asset manager's decisions.
- **Project Construction Management**
  Project construction management governs the improvement of the asset quality by managing the suppliers.
- **Facility Management**
  Facility management looks after cleaning and doorman services.

The most important property-management company in Italy is Prelios (www.prelios.com), an asset- and fund-management company that is responsible for promoting, establishing, and managing investment funds. It also has a stake in the consultancy business, in which it provides advice to national and international investors concerning superior real estate strategies. Founded in 2003, Prelios has established itself as one of the dominant companies in the Italian real estate industry. The company comprises 130 national and international investors, including pension funds, insurance companies, financial institutions, foundations, and sovereign funds.

Developers

Developers buy land and build assets.

CityLife

CityLife (www.city-life.it) is a commercial, residential, and business district that is under construction near the old city center in Milan. It is approximately 36.6 hectares in size. The Generali Group is developing the site, which has been designed by some of the most well-known architects, including Japan's Arata Isozaki, Anglo-Iraqi architect Zaha Hadid, and Daniel Libeskind. Artistic management plays a very important role in real estate development. The main architect firms in Italy are Michele De Lucchi (www.amdl.it), whose staff developed Il Centro in Arese; Metrogramma (www.metrogramma.com), whose staff developed Scalo Milano; Arcoretail (www.arcotecnicagroup.com); and Faver (www.fm-ingegneria.com).

The CityLife project completely changed the Milan skyline with its three skyscrapers:

- **Il Dritto (The Straight One)**
  In 2016, Emporis (www.emporis.com) nominated Il Dritto as the third-best skyscraper in the world. Il Dritto (or Allianz Tower) is currently one of the tallest buildings in Italy. With its broadcast antenna and its fifty floors, it is the tallest if you count the roof. Isozaki designed it in collaboration with Italian architect Andrea Maffei.

  The tower comprises eight modules of six floors each. The facade of these modules comprises a triple glass unit that is slightly curved to the outside. The vertical succession of rounded forms creates an effect of vibration as the building rises upward. Its short sides are fully glazed to show the mechanical series of panoramic lifts going up and down to its various floors. The idea of an endless tower can be attributed to the ambitions of other artists—Constantin Brancusi, for instance, who from 1937–1938 installed one of his endless columns of Targu-Jiu in the park to create indefinite, repeated systems.

Today, Il Dritto serves as the headquarters of the Allianz Group and its Italian parent company, Allianz S.p.A.

- **Lo Storto (The Twisted One)**

Lo Storto (or Generali Tower) is 185 meters high; it has forty-four floors, combined with three basement floors, and a total floor area of about sixty-seven thousand square meters. It was designed by Hadid.

The geometry of the building is that of a warping shape, where both the floors' dimensions and their orientations vary along the tower's axis. The structure is concrete and composite. A horizontal central core acts as its main stiffening and resisting element. Foundations are made of mixed raft and piles type, where the piles are used as settlement-reduction devices. The base raft is a 2.5-meter-thick concrete slab resting on sixty-four piles (arranged in clusters) and points under the main load points. In order to resist the torsional effects from the warped-column arrangement, the core lintels above the structure's main doors feature composite solutions with a mixture of steel elements, rebar, and concrete. Due to the specific form-dependent deformation effects, a highly sophisticated stage analysis, both for construction and long-term effects, has been affected. A steel, free-form podium for commercial use surrounds the base of the building.

Lo Storto serves as the headquarters of Assicurazioni Generali, the second-largest (by revenue) insurance group in the world.

- **Il Curvo (The Curved One)**

  Il Curvo will be 175 meters high, with twenty-eight floors and a total floor area of about seventy-six thousand square meters. Situated between Il Dritto and Lo Storto, the structure will slope in toward its counterparts and the Piazza Tre Torri below.

  The Renaissance cupola is the basic principle behind Il Curvo's concept. It is reinterpreted through the concave movement of its elevation, and it culminates in the crown, both distinctive elements of the building. The curved tower's facade is made of sustainable, state-of-the-art glass that will reflect the public space below and surrounding vistas.

  Il Curvo will serve as the headquarters of the Intesa Sanpaolo bank.

Hines

A global real estate development, investment, and management firm with offices in twenty countries and 192 cities, Hines (www.hines.com) is currently managing $93 billion worth of assets. They also provide $47.9 billion in fiduciary investment management services as well as $45.3 billion for third-party property-level services. The company is in the process of constructing 105 developments around the globe, having previously redeveloped or secured 1,180 properties. Its current portfolio includes 483 properties. Of course, Hines is known as one of the largest and most respected real estate companies in the world.

Hines was the biggest investor in the Italian property market in 2016, with a €700 million investment, and it intends to increase its investments in 2017. Lars Huber, Hines's CEO in Europe, has said that the company's major focus is on high-quality central properties, which are risk free, as they do not lose value even in the face of political instability or economic crisis.

In 2016, Hines experienced periods of uncertainty as a result of the British and Italian referendums in addition to the United States' presidential election. Hines's strategy is to continue to invest while still seeking other higher-quality investments in better locations. The company is best known for developing Milan's Porta Nuova area, which reinvented the Lombardy capital. Today, Italy continues to play an important role in Hines's long-term strategy.

General Contractors

The general contractor is a manager (and possibly a tradesman) employed by the client on the advice of the architect, engineer or architectural technologist, though the client can also act as the manager. A general contractor is responsible for the overall coordination of a project and must first assess the project-specific documents, referred to as bid, proposal, or tender documents. In the case of renovations, the contractor will visit the site to get a better understanding of the project. Depending on the project's delivery method, he or she will submit a fixed-price proposal or bid, a cost-plus price, or an estimate.

The general contractor typically considers the cost of home office overhead, general conditions, materials, and equipment, as well as the cost of labor, to provide the owner with a total price for the project. Contract documents include drawings, the project manual (including general, supplementary, and/or special conditions and specifications), and any addendums or modifications issued prior to the proposal or bidding. They are prepared by a design professional, such as an architect. The general contractor may be the construction manager or construction manager at risk.

The leading contractors active in commercial real estate in Italy today include the Percassi Group (www.percassi.it)—the main building company in the retail sector—Colombo (www.colombocostruizioni.eu), *CMB (www.cmbcarpi.it)*, and Rizzani De Eccher (www.rizzanideeccher.com).

Pure Service Providers

Pure service providers offer property-management and advisory services but do not own any assets.

Cushman & Wakefield
Cushman & Wakefield is a world-renowned global real estate services firm. The array of services offered range from corporate finance and investment banking to property management, valuation, and advisory.

Jones Lang LaSalle Incorporated (JLL)
Jones Lang LaSalle is a professional and financial advisory organization that specializes in real estate services and capital management. It has been labeled a Fortune 500 company on account of its global sales of more than $6 billion. The span of its services enables JLL to meet the needs of clients locally, regionally, and globally. It currently has an investment portfolio worth $59.7 billion. The company is headquartered in the Aon Center in Chicago, Illinois.

The company has about fifty-three thousand employees, including professional and support staff. It also has more than 230 offices worldwide, in eighty countries. JLL's global revenue was $4 billion in 2014, and the firm now has a portfolio of three billion square feet under management. After the CBRE Group, it is the largest publicly traded commercial real estate brokerage firm in the world. Apart from Cushman & Wakefield, its other competitors include DTZ, Cassidy Turley, Colliers International, and Newmark Grubb Knight Frank. In 2016, for the ninth consecutive year, the Ethisphere Institute named JLL one of the world's most ethical companies.

Private Equity
Real estate investment funds are common instruments of investment in real estate assets, particularly for institutional investors. Introduced in Italy in 1994, real estate funds are effective in the management of savings and characterized by the investment of at least two-thirds of the assets in real estate properties, beneficial real estate property rights, and stakes in real estate companies. Based on the subscription of the shares, whether they are in liquidity or through means of asset contribution, the real estate funds can be distinguished by ordinary

funds or contribution funds. They may also offer a distribution of proceeds or their accumulation until the fund matures. Legislation limits the assumption of debt on behalf of the real estate fund to 60 percent on the value of real estate properties, beneficial real estate property rights, and stakes in real estate companies, and to 20 percent on the value of other assets.

An Italian real estate investment fund is considered a closed-end alternative investment fund (AIF). In other words, it is founded and directed by a manager for use as a separate pool of assets, split into units and collected through an assortment of units. When more than one investor is involved, the units are managed as a whole, in the interest of the unit holders, and then individually. Investment in real estate is typically made on the basis of a predetermined investment policy. An Italian real estate investment fund whose units are available for purchase or subscription exclusively by those investors identified by the decree of the Ministry of Finance, or by professional investors, is referred to as "reserved."

The entities involved in the management of real estate funds are as follows:

- **Asset-Management Companies (SGRs)**
  The Società di Gestione del Risparmio (SGR) defines the management policy guidelines contained in the fund's management regulation and is responsible for the investment, management, and disposition of the fund's assets as well as the coordination of the activities conferred to outsourcing partners, including property management, facility management, and agency services. A reserved real estate investment fund can be set up and managed through an Italian management company incorporated into the SGR, which holds a license from the bank of Italy, or through an entity that has been authorized by a European member state.

  As of January 2017, Italy has 139 SGRs, with a trend toward reduction. Usually, SGRs are not suitable for assets under management lower than €2 billion due to the management costs related to the company. Out of the 139 SGRs, twenty-two of them are currently active in real estate, managing 228 real estate funds. Out of the 228 real estate funds, twenty are retail funds.

The first SGRs in Italy were IDeA FIMIT (www.ideafimit. it), Generali (www.generali-immobiliare.it), Prelios (www. preliossgr.com), and BNP (www.reim.bnpparibas.it). They account for 62 percent of the total market.

- **Depository Banks**
  The depository bank is responsible for the custody of the financial instruments and liquidity of the fund.

- **Independent Surveyors**
  Independent surveyors are professional service providers. Every six months, they prepare and issue valuations on those real estate properties, beneficial real estate property rights, and stakes in real estate companies in which the fund invests.

- **Supervisory Entities and Authorities**
  Banca d'Italia, Consob, and Borsa Italiana; an auditing firm; and the SGR's board of statutory auditors preside over the system of supervisory controls relative to the real estate funds.

Italian reserved real estate investment funds should be managed in line with a predetermined investment policy, and that policy must invest capital of an amount equal to a minimum of two-thirds of their entire value in (1) real estate assets, (2) REM rights for real estate assets, (3) real estate company equity interests, and (4) other real estate AIFs. It must also invest all remaining capital, or one-third of their total value, into assets that are legally permissible. Reserved real estate investment funds are not directly permitted to carry out any building activity.

Investors take part in real estate funds by purchasing or subscribing units. Numerous unit classes can be issued as long as investors who subscribe the same unit class are provided the same duties and powers.

An Italian SICAF is a closed-end AIF managed by the UFA and the AIFMD. It is set up as a joint stock company (S.p.A.) with fixed capital and a registered office located in Italy, having as its exclusive corporate purpose the investment of the assets collected through the issue of shares or other equity instruments, among several investors, managed as a whole in the interest of its investors and independently from them. It is invested mainly in real estate on the basis of a predetermined investment policy. SICAFs are typically subject to the same regulations provided for other AIFs, and the Bank of Italy must authorize the establishment of a SICAF.

Private equity real estate is a class of investable assets that consists of equity and debt investments within the property markets, allowing multiple investors to combine their funds.

Traditionally, investing in private-equity real estate requires long-term consideration. It also requires an active management strategy and significant upfront capital commitment to a fund that seeks potential investment opportunities in the space. Little flexibility is offered to investors, as the capital commitment needs several years; however, given that real estate is popular as an asset class, it provides high levels of potential income with strong future price appreciation.

Core
Core investing is the safest form of real estate investing. It involves the buying and holding of stable assets defined by their low vacancies, high quality, relative location, and strong markets.

Typically, core investors prefer yield over appreciation and view real estate as a comparatively safe place to invest capital. This investment approach can be considered an alternative to bonds—with the added benefit of being backed by a physical asset—and can offer a potential hedge against inflation. The average targeted internal rate of return (IRR) will usually be below 10 percent.

Despite the recent high prices for CRE assets creating some concern as to core investments, 50 percent of private equity real estate investors intend to continue pursuing the strategy.

Core Plus

Core plus funds give investors the opportunity to invest in real estate vehicles of moderate risk that provide moderate returns. These funds adopt a value-added approach to some extent, but investments are mostly core in nature. Like core vehicles, core plus funds target class-A properties that need some sort of improvement. These vehicles generally use leverage of between 30 percent and 55 percent and provide a less risky alternative to value-added and opportunistic funds.

Value Added

Higher risk is associated with value-added strategies. These investments generally include properties that have a considerable execution risk to add the necessary value to drive enhanced returns, such as repositioning, major renovation, or lease-up to stabilization.

Value-added investors typically look to keep an asset for five to seven years, which gives them enough time to launch their strategy. They understand that much of their return will come from appreciation over yield. This strategy is predicated on the idea that adding some initial value can lead to outsized returns upon disposition.

Leasing is often considered a major part of a value-added strategy. A good brokerage team will market effectively, attract worthy tenants, and negotiate competitive deals to drive up the value at time of disposition. This approach was expected to be the most popular in 2016, when 55 percent of private-equity real estate investors were planning to pursue value-added investments. Investors are drawn to this strategy because it allows them to escape the competitive prices for prime assets in gateway markets.

Opportunistic

The highest risk-reward investment strategy is the opportunistic approach. Investors pursuing this strategy generally look for properties that need a considerable amount of work, whether because of renovation needs, high vacancy, or relative strength of the market. New development is often included in this category, too. Due to the amount of work that needs to be invested in restoring the property, it can yield the highest returns, but it also involves the greatest level of risk. Such assets are typically held for three to seven years, with the goal of achieving a 15 percent plus IRR.

Real estate funds listed in Italy total forty-five billion of gross asset value (GAV) or thirty-two billion of net asset value (NAV), or net of debt. The average leverage is 35 percent. Real estate funds invest 42 percent in offices, 20 percent in the residential sector, 14 percent in retail, and 3 percent in logistics (though that final percentage is growing).

Since the outbreak of the global financial crisis in 2007–2008, an entire group of opportunistic American investors have swooped in on Europe in search of cheap assets and nonperforming loans. Cerberus and Lone Star have headed the hunt for distressed loan portfolios, while Blackstone has broadened its horizon and picked up corporations like Dutch retail specialist Multi, which it acquired by taking control of the company's debt. Since then, Blackstone has consolidated its retail presence across Europe and established a sturdy logistics platform. In 2016, the private equity giant raised $6.3 billion in the second closing of its new fund, Blackstone Real Estate Partners Europe V (BREP V). The fund is expected to invest the majority of its capital in the five European economies: Germany, the United Kingdom, France, Italy, and Spain.

4

REAL ESTATE RISKS IN ITALY

During the last decade, the finance sector has integrated with the real estate sector, and this has led to several positive outcomes. For instance, the merger has generated role awareness in retail operators, who in turn have improved the overall culture of real estate valuation by using valuation methods that conform to international standards. It has also produced training and strong growth.

As the finance sector begins to intensify its role within the real estate sector, the lending institutions responsible for developing and implementing the transparent procedures for evaluating real estate assets, also used to secure credit, are highly rewarded. In 2010, a significant trend in Italy led to the publication of precise guidelines for asset valuation in terms of real estate in small areas that have a high environmental and tourist value—destinations like Costa Smeralda. The value of real estate in such areas is prone to rise in value, especially when it comes to high-end properties. A lot of the time, the unit value for real estate in these locations can be greater than more superior segments in the world's largest capital cities. Foreign investors, who have established major residential developments and tourist attractions on the foundation of the virtue of the local natural environment, have influenced the development of this type of area.

An evaluation of real estate investment risk should take into account a wide range of factors that are not always related to the asset's quality. In fact, it should include factors that are especially difficult to pinpoint and study. When real estate investment risk is being analyzed, the main focus should be on whether the property can preserve the environmental features that made the location so successful in the first place. The relationship between the total value of the estate and the value directly related to its external characteristics—such as the quality of the building and its environmental context—should also be considered. The first is determined through the study of those local elements responsible for driving the value of the area and by establishing which factors have the potential to cause those elements to devalue. The second is assessed by determining the coefficient of the relationship between market value and embedded value. The latter highlights the percentage of the value that is stable within the building relative to its market value.

The main three risks to consider when developing real estate in Italy are as follows:

- **Urbanistic Risk**
  It may take a long time to obtain a permit from public authorities.
- **Building Risk**
  Development costs may increase over time, or budgeted amounts may change due to time delays.
- **Market Risk**
  It may be difficult to sell the assets if the market is adverse.

The Bersani-Visco Law

The purpose of the Bersani-Visco law is to prevent tax evasion, a very common practice in the residential real estate market in Italy. Upon its enactment, it led to a number of deals being delayed, lots of savings being lost, and many investors—particularly international ones—pulling their funds out of the market. Moreover, all efforts the

Italian real estate industry made to build a market to attract global investment vanished. The Bersani-Visco law has essentially made the Italian real estate industry much less competitive.

Recovery has become increasingly difficult, and many Italian companies have decided to invest in foreign markets instead. Fortunately, the property funds sector continues to grow in terms of numbers and power. Within a few years of the law's enactment, more than eighty property funds were launched, managed by more than forty asset-management companies, for a total value of €20 billion. And there is still plenty of room for growth. The current national stock of property is estimated at more than €4 trillion.

In 2007, new confidence surfaced in the industry with the introduction of the Italian REITs. At the time, research centers around the country stated that SIIQs could boast more than €50 billion within twenty-four months.

CONCLUSION

From its architecture and art to its food and wine, from its language and landscape to its vivacious people and their joy of life, for thousands of years Italy has been perfecting the things it is best known for.

It is the country's ageless charm that inspires foreign investment. When it is combined with a multitude of cheap properties and a favorable currency rate, for dollar or sterling, buyers in particular are seeing that Italy's present climate makes this the best time to dive into real estate. Italian and foreign investors alike are looking at the market with renewed interest.

Experts predict that prices should stay level for a time; they don't see any substantial drops or buildups on the horizon. The market is experiencing many investors' return to Italy's lasting trusted locations. At the peak of the market, buyers are looking at areas such as Abruzzo and Le Marche to get greater value for their money. As overall prices have declined since 2009, they are now recessing at 30 percent below their best. Lucca, Pisa, Chianti, Cortona, and many of the hilltop villages are now picking up in pace. Either investors are drawn to locations like Tuscany, with its Renaissance-style architecture and rolling hills, or they fall in love with Umbria, with its mountainous Etruscan landscapes. There seems to be a narrowing in the price gap between the two locations.

Lifestyle will always be the main reason why people choose to invest in Italy, but their purchase should also have a commercial goal. Accordingly, investors often look for properties with rental potential to ensure that their costs are covered. They also look for properties, whether urban or rural, that do not require any major work. New, high-quality build projects remain scarce in Italy; however, there is a demand for lock-up-and-leave apartments in Rome, Florence, Milan, and Venice. Owners can typically expect a rental season of twenty-two to twenty-five weeks for a property that is newly renovated and well located.

The economic crisis has certainly had a negative effect on the Italian economy during the last few years. Despite its financial collapse, the Italian real estate market has maintained stability in terms of value, even though a reduction in sales—especially in larger cities—has revealed a limit in risk. A decline in sales in no way indicates that the market has come to a standstill. In fact, corporate companies have made some substantial investments and development plans, and they plan to continue to do so.

Even if the Italian real estate market lacks the dynamic nature of other European markets in terms of its structure, the last ten years have seen a positive trend involving institutional investors playing active roles in real estate investment funds. This has resulted in a stabilization of the market, making it more effective and transparent.

As is the case in any country, it is important for a foreign investor that wants to reach its investment goals to have good local partners, whether that be an independent advisor or a resident associate who provides active support throughout the investment process.

Political and economic stability is the basis for the Italian real estate market's continued recovery. The contribution and role of regional policy is specifically needed to counter the structural weakness of the country's economy.

Today, Italy is still the eighth-largest economy in the world. Nevertheless, going forward, many improvements must be made for the country to continue to compete effectively in the global market.

Although the economy is not expected to return to its precrisis real output peak until the mid-2020s, it still has some potential. To enhance the competitiveness of its economy, Italy will have to enact comprehensive structural reforms. In particular, it needs to promote growth with countercyclical fiscal policies while preserving macro stability, and by further diversifying its economy. The country also needs to reform a paralyzed legislative system. These are just a few of the initiatives that would boost the economy, which in turn would attract more foreign investment.

Experts say that 2017 is the best time to invest in real estate because the market is currently set at a healthy medium. Italy will remain a highly active tourist market, which will always make Italian properties an attractive prospect. On a national level, rental prospects likewise look good because an increasing number of tourists want to stay in rural locations. This is a good time for investors who are looking to turn old Italian houses into stylish modern dwellings. The most important thing to remember, however, is that Italy has no capital gains or wealth tax, and this makes it a very viable prospect in terms of lucrative property investment.

ABOUT THE AUTHOR

Gabriele Fraschini has more than twenty years of management experience, including ten years with a Big Four firm. He is currently finance director of a real estate company backed by a private-equity investor. Gabriele has a strong background in business transformation, including delocalization, shared services, postmerger integration, and ERP implementation. He has served in various senior financial and corporate development positions with private and listed companies in a variety of industries.